Offline Poet

poetry by nikki van ekeren

Cover art and layout by Matt Van Ekeren

Imprint: Independently published

For information regarding permission or distribution, contact nikkivanekeren@gmail.com

To discover more about the author visit nikkivanekeren.com

ISBN: 978-1-7355066-5-4

van ekeren

Going offline to exist, even if just for the moment, elevates your energy and helps you realign with yourself.

You seem to come home to yourself.

This pure and simple space is always available.

This book is a reflection of the feelings that I uncovered when I went offline, when I let myself feel it all. I hope to continue this quest.

Will you join me?

Do you accept the adventure of being you?

chapter 1
coming home

1. the freedom offline	12
2. fear as the creative fuel	14
3. dancing with the discomfort	15
4. to generate meaning	16
5. coming home to yourself	18
6. how to measure your success	20
7. when everything just feels special	22
8. it is all okay	25
9. from prison to possibilities	26
10. feeling that inner sass	28
11. conscious intention	30
12. underneath	33
13. toward yourself	34
14. just be simple	35
15. home is inside	36

chapter 2
she

1. she knows	40
2. she seeks wonder	42
3. she is the artist of her life	43
4. getting there	44
5. her promise to herself	46
6. she	47
7. she believes	49
8. she knows herself	50
9. she defies the norm	51

10. her work   52

11. she is one of those people   54

12. she always lives in the summer   56

13. she used to   58

chapter 3

poet in residence

1. poet in residence   62

2. the design of it all   65

3. write a thank you letter to yourself   66

4. know your why   69

5. pain becomes art   70

6. the force that animates you   72

7. you are never missing out   74

8. plant the seeds   75

9. when you stop ignoring   76

10. offline poet   78

chapter 4

blue jean era

1. blue jean era   82

2. just be open to it all   83

3. the simplicity of focus   84

4. infuse courage   87

5. developing self reverence   88

6. that casual cool vibe in jeans and a t-shirt   90

7. just knowing   92

8. the flicker of something new   93

9. your favorite t-shirt   94

10. yesterday happened so today could   96

11. the work of sadness   98

12. the perfect wave   100

chapter 5

she speaks in poems

1. she speaks in poems   104

2. she is waking up to herself   105

3. she's an old soul poet   106

4. her imagination   108

5. engage in new material   109

6. she will not settle   110

7. she is poetry   113

8. the lure of the inner critic   114

9. she meets herself   116

10. poetry is   118

11. she gets lost in art   120

12. just start enjoying it all   122

13. momentum is life   125

14. face it   126

15. let your decisions guide you   127

chapter 6

life is a mood board

1. let your life be a mood board   130

2. trust your art   131

3. the beginning   132

4. honor your entire being   133

5. keep creating it   134

6. thriving is contagious   135

7. sharing your heart   137

8. the life of an observer   138

9. patience and momentum   140

10. the now   141

11. writing the script   142

12. back in the flow of it all   143

14. to create from peace   144

chapter 7
to romanticize life

1. always young   149

2. when your inner compass speaks   150

3. the version of you   151

4. seeing life as a poem   152

5. style is what you are   154

6. your story   155

7. brooklyn breeze   156

8. your life   157

9. the moments   158

10. your response   160

11. golden hour   162

12. intentionally iconic   163

13. letting life love you   164

14. to romanticize life   166

van ekeren

chapter one

coming home

the freedom offline

when you untangle yourself
from the confines of the digital universe,
you fall back into the magic of it all.
the anxious tendencies you felt
to become something else
vanish immediately.
you are alone,
yet surrounded by your complete essence.

journeying offline
means disconnecting to the
incessant noise of the day.
it means listening
and being a part of the moment.
as you unplug and choose
to be out in the world,
you absorb life in an intentional way.

the thoughts within
and the sounds around you
all have an uplifting and inspiring tone.
the symphony of life sounds so sweet.
you are here
in this moment.

the choice to disconnect
seemingly connects you
deeper to yourself
and the world around you.
the inner battle
slowly resolves itself
and you are in alignment.
you feel your youthful innocence
and naivety resurface.
you have found
what you were searching for.

fear as the creative fuel

let fear become the catalyst,
not the stop sign.
let fear ignite your creativity,
rather than stifle it.

memorize the feeling of courage
and practice it.
when fear makes its presence known,
react how you want to.
feel into this new response.

allow curiosity to be your new lens
into the fear.
it is not about eliminating the fear
rather it is about navigating through it
as the person that you want to be.

dancing with the discomfort

you thought you needed to heal completely
to feel safe and happy.
what if you learned how to dance with it all?
what if you leaned into
the uncomfortable moments?
you are a continual work in progress.
life is about getting creative
with the energetic nature of fear.
you cannot escape it,
yet you can dance with it.
you can alchemize it
and turn it into something magical.
you are a beautiful being
dancing with it all.

to generate meaning

when you get the inner calling
to change some of your deep rooted beliefs,
your entire life shifts.
this inner nudge has shown you how
seeds were planted
in the fertile soil of your brain
that have sprouted into painful narratives.
you can see how
the vast environment of your childhood
left you with limiting beliefs
that held you back and caused fear.
your entire identity feels shaken
with this realization.

face the responses that arise
and then pause with them.
clarity takes rational thinking and patience.
your initial response to change
will feel frenetic and heavy.
you will feel weighed down
by this overwhelming truth.
keep feeling.
you are embarking on the greatest upheaval
and revival of your life.

you are uprooting the weeds
and replacing them with hope.
you are generating new meaning to your
entire existence.
at this point,
everything feels more intense
and magnified.
you may feel forgetful and a bit scared.
your authentic responses are natural.
now, you get to collaborate
with the unseen forces
that swirl within and around you.
this is the most exciting time
of your life so far.

harness the human
that you know you will become
and then go act as her.
transform into this person
in your mind.
character is destiny,
not your old beliefs.
become the artist of
your beautiful burgeoning character.

coming home to yourself

making the leap
to return to yourself
can happen in an instant.
it is a moment that has taken years
to arrive at.
it is the result
of intentional work.
the pursuit of being able to see in the dark,
to observe yourself without judgment
and to identify what no longer works.

you used to naively flow
with the trends of the culture.
now, you are developing more discernment
and self awareness.
you are able to hear
the calling of your soul.
the signals and messages
are more clear now.
you long to come home to yourself.

you know that the journey
will be challenging and uncomfortable.
you have worked hard to build some things
that you may have to tear down.

you accept it all.
you get to be you
and come home to yourself
for the rest of your life.

how to measure your success

learn how to measure your success
with intentionality and kindness.
rather than wait for your inner world
to be perfect and calm,
just declare that it is.
allow the words from your ego
to exist as they must,
knowing that you do not need to fight it.
you have decided to be happy
and that you shall be.
understand that the ego
has evolved over many years
and is brilliant at trying to take you down.
pause, to breathe in and refresh
your inner hardware.
you own this hardware
while the ego can be the running software.
you get to reboot, refresh
and restart at any time.
let this action be your victory.
know that this precious and subtle restraint
is changing your life.
you are not intimidated, you are liberated.

**you get to be you
and come home to yourself
for the rest of your life.**

when everything just feels special

coming home to yourself
means confronting the ego that you've created.
this ego may mistakenly feel like home,
yet will distract you
from feeling like your purest self.
the ego that is trying to get you to think
of yesterday's mistakes
rather than today's possibilities.
when you awaken
to the never ending upkeep of the ego,
you can disassociate from its grasp.
the ego will always have an opinion,
but you do not have to get tangled
up in its web.

when you observe it
rather than identify with it,
life feels so special.
you are honored to be living it.
you are touched by your humanness
and laugh at your mistakes.
after all,
you get to be here.
you get to be the version of you
that you are creating in real time.
you are an amazing work of art.

when you can stop fighting your ego,
you can come home to yourself again.
that voice that wants to control
your inner narrative,
is no longer a foe.
you are at peace with its pull.
you know how to observe it
rather than be it.
you can now live in
your true energetic self—
that expansive feeling within
that is full of harmony,
acceptance and momentum.
this inner alignment fuels a life
that feels good to live.

**you are here
in real time
trying your best.
go you!**

it is all okay

just remember
when you make a mistake
and seem to have let yourself down,
that it is all okay.
you are human
and will always be adjusting
your inner world
to outside stimulus.
it is okay
if you slip up.
this is a feature of your personality
not a defect.
your awareness of your mistakes
shows that you are growing.
you can then
reframe how you think of these mistakes.
they are not shameful incidents,
rather they are proof that you
are participating openly in your life.
you are here
in real time
trying your best.
go you!

from prison to possibilities

you used to think that your mind
felt like a prison.
one tied to your ego
ready to deliver messages
of why you should feel
shame, regret or doubt.
day after day,
the voice
clamored for your attention,
digging deeper and deeper
and more personal with each accusation.
then, you paused and observed it.
you watched it rather than respond to it.
you could see it as a separate entity—
a thinking device that has the ability
to help or harm you at any time.
you unlocked the door to this so-called prison
and walked out.
life is completely different now.
the ego has not stopped its devastating words,
but those words are not something for you to
stop or control.
you just need to control how you react
to the ego's attempts.
you understand that vital inner tools

are always available.
when you can identify how the ego is trying
to fool you,
you can use the right tools
to work through it.
let it all become effortless
and let yourself soar.

feeling that inner sass

there comes a time
when you stop worrying
about everyone else
and start allowing your fullest self
to emerge.
you feel that inner sass again.
you feel the youthful spirit
that wants you to soar
rather than hold back
for anyone or anything.
the clarity in
your vision and thoughts
has returned.

feeling that inner sass again
feels so good.
you are grateful
for the journey that led you here
and have no regrets.
you needed to navigate the challenging terrain
to come home again.
you know
that the role of a lifetime
is being yourself.
you understand how special you are.

you know yourself fully
and will continue
writing this beautiful character
in real time.

conscious intention

your conscious intention
is more powerful than unconscious fear.
remember,
that you are not
similar to one of pavlov's dogs.
you are not as programmable
as you have been led to believe.

you are able to think in the moment
and distinguish between the present,
the past
and the future.
you are not sleepwalking through life,
rather you are alive and aware.

do not be scared by fear.
face it.
own up to it.
look at it with deep awareness.
consciously choose to keep moving forward.
even if you have to pretend
to be courageous,
do it.
this intentional approach
is your tool.

you will succeed
because you have laid out the way
to do so.

your unconscious fears
seem to swirl about and strike at random.
instead of feeling scared,
just notice them.
remind yourself that you
can get through anything.
you are merging with the future self
that you are consciously creating.
she is you.
you are her.
and, she is amazing!

32

**just be more simple.
put the phone down for the day
and play.**

underneath

underneath the surface of fear
is excitement for change and growth.
rather than work to protect yourself
from this feeling,
embrace it.
learn how to exist in this space
of discomfort.
it is your training ground
to become the person
that you've always dreamed of being.
you will never be able to completely
eliminate fear.
it is part of the human experience.
lean into it.
celebrate it.
it's your sign that you are doing the work.
you are jumping into life
and living!
redefine fear
as excitement
and commit to this perspective.
savor this initiative.
continue to focus.
your life is going to be
your ongoing reward.

toward yourself

keep moving
toward yourself.
keep discovering
what makes you
feel more like you.
as you grow more empowered
in your skin,
share your ways
with the world.
encourage yourself
as you encourage others.
feel the feelings you want to experience
within your body.
create the things
that you want to see in the world.
feel spacious,
sassy,
safe
and secure
just because you're you.

just be simple

sometimes, it helps to remember
how simple life can be.
imagine your younger self
and what your days looked like then.
what did you seek out?
by setting this intention to be more simple,
you may change goals and expectations.
reframe your dreams to be in sync
with who you are now.

just be more simple.
put the phone down for the day
and play.
get silly and laugh out loud.
enjoy your own company.
seek out joy
and love
and wander until you feel it.
you may not have to go that far
because you will find these things within.

home is inside

coming home
to the space inside.
the safe space that you had to separate
yourself from for a bit.
you are not sure why,
but you felt a pull to do so.
the outside world
felt more special
than your inner world.
you journeyed toward a distant light
only to discover that the light source has
always been generated from within.
you are the person
that you have always been looking for.
you hold all the answers,
the love
and the strength that you will ever need.
you are it.
home is inside.

**coming home
to the space inside.**

chapter two

she

she knows

she began to see
personal transformation
as a bold and luxurious act.
rather than hide her joy of growth,
she now shares her transformation
with audacity.

she knows that personal inquiry
is a coveted journey.
her sincere and empathetic nature
is a gift.

she wears her wisdom
as she wears her jewelry—
with pride, style and dignity.
she is not afraid anymore
of the thoughts that do not feel good.
her courageous approach
to her inner world
gives her clarity and focus.
inner alignment and peace
is her goal.

she knows who she is
and is honored to share her story.

she adores who she has become
and feels reverence for who she was.
every moment
has sculpted her soul
and shaped her heart.

she continues
to choose happiness.
this makes every other choice simple.
she knows that inner peace and growth
are the ultimate luxuries.
she is just getting started.

she seeks wonder

she longs to see the beauty
that is always around her.
she seeks art
because it keeps her timeless.
she lets things come easy to her
because this is how it is supposed to be.
she romanticizes her life
in real time
and infuses poetry into
every fiber of her being.
in the midst of pain,
she doesn't fight it, she embraces it.
she is not scared of anything.
she celebrates herself
and never waits for another to do it for her.
she is the keeper of her fate
and understands
that her character will inform this.
the wonder of love and kindness
still intrigue her.
she seeks beauty in the world
and always finds it.
she trusts that she will always wonder
with reverence.

she is the artist of her life

she is creating her most
important masterpiece—
her life.
this requires focus,
drive
and direction.
she understands that
certain unhealthy habits and patterns
may pop up
and try to shape her.
she has identified when
these inner patterns arise
and knows how to quiet them.
they are not to be feared.
they just are part of living
the human experience.
she is the artist of her life
and has chosen to create everything
within and around her.
each small detail is as important
as its large counterpart.
she finds this entire process divine
and full of possibilites.
after all, she is creating herself
in real time.

getting there

she always has a way
of getting to where she needs to be.
she is not calculated
rather she is tapped into something.
she listens to cues from the universe.
she makes decisions and sticks to them.

her style of life is not for everyone
and others have let her know.
she may not fit in,
but this does not deter her.
she knows who she is.
she is certain that she will get there
wherever "there" may be.

she abides to the map within
and loves to keep moving.
this may mean a few wrong turns
here and there.
she slowly navigates
the terrain of life
allowing the wrong turns
to lead to something fun.

getting there
is about wandering
and discovering.
she is driven by something deep inside
and is not out to prove herself to anyone.
her momentum feeds her
and her choices continue to thrill her.

her promise to herself

as she became more aware
and able to observe herself
with an objective lens,
she could understand more.
she could see how she had given over
her power to generate love.
the trauma she had endured
provoked her to abandon herself
in order to gain external love.
she remembered that to observe something
is to be able to dance with it.
she decided to dance with it all—
the pain, joy and everything in between.

she made a promise to herself
to create unconditional love from within.
she would merge with her own love
rather than work for another's.
this sacred vow to herself
opened up her world in magical ways.
her love for herself continues to grow.
she is able to see herself
as capable, strong, independent
and as an icon.

she

she gets to be
the woman
that she wants to be.
she gets to let go
of the pain
that others inflicted upon her.
she gets to learn
how to see the truth
and live it.
she gets to thrive
and soar
because she chose to let go of shame.
she is merging with her beautiful destiny
and letting her past go.
she gets to be exactly who she is today
because of what happened yesterday.
rather than focus on the other characters
in the story,
she focuses on herself,
the main character.

**she gets to be exactly
who she is today
because of what happened
yesterday.**

she believes

she believes in herself
and understands that no one else
can do this work for her.
she champions her voice.
it is clear that
she must believe in herself first
and then invite others in
for the ride.
this momentum,
this force
and this form of self trust
propels her life forward in the right direction.

she knows herself

she knows what ignites her soul.
she understands that when she feels
more like herself,
she feels free.
she is vulnerable in this pure joy
and happily exists in it.
this pure form of happiness
within the world
is her ultimate creation.
the subtle nuances involved
in order to feel this freedom
will be a lifelong exploration.
her fiery focus fuels her life forward.
her work is to fearlessly
continue this growth.

she defies the norm

she is her biggest cheerleader
and believes in herself.
this is vital for someone
who chooses to live in a truly authentic space.
she works to understand herself,
rather than understand the latest trends.
she knows that she is on the journey
of a lifetime to be herself.
she only says yes
to the things that she wants to do.
she never compares herself to another
because she is so happy
creating her own things.
she doesn't look to anyone
to make her happy.
she knows that the most valuable fortune
is what you make for yourself.

her work

she decided to do the work
on her own
and not ask for the world to notice.
she got quiet.
she became focused
and intentional
about herself,
her journey
and her boundaries.
at first
it felt lonely,
but then it felt new and exciting and full.
now, she is exuding
her own true essence.
she is herself.

she decided to do the work.

she is one of those people

she's just one of those people
that the world
cannot harm.
she does not accept
the culture's norms
or judgements
or expectations.
she knows her value
and chooses to
flex that muscle.
she truly lives.

when she feels anxiety
or pain
or anything that doesn't feel good,
she chooses to sit with it.
rather than run,
she pauses.
she feels it thoroughly
and does not hide from it.
she celebrates
her ability
to be honest with herself.

55

life can be challenging,
but she knows that
difficulty is a mindset.
if she labels it as easy,
she can learn how to make it so.
she is just one of those people.

she always lives in the summer

she measures her life
through summers.
feeling like each day
could last forever
because she feels so present.
watching the sunset paint the sky
with the people she loves.
letting the air touch her skin
while wearing her favorite fits.
letting the warmth of the sun
slow her down
because there is nowhere to rush to.
seeking it all out,
yet settling in and relaxing.
letting the weather
be part of her story.
allowing the summer magic
to speak through her.
enjoying the lack of routine
that her summer months evoke.
she may meet up with a friends
or take a day to be quiet and solo.
her favorite activity is
just soaking up
the ability to wander for no reason.
she is always in that summer mood.

**she measures her life
through summers.**

she used to

she used to listen
to everyone else
but herself.
this was not always the case,
but as life progressed
she lost a sense of inner alignment
and turned to others for a sense of self.
blame it on her circumstances,
her lack of tools
or her relationships,
this blame does not help.
she realized this
and focused on the present moment.
for this moment
is the only space
where lasting change can happen.
she used to run from her truth,
now, she to runs toward it.
at first, it was dark.
she was not sure if she could handle it.
soon, she discovered that she was able
and equipped to do anything.
her present, past and future self
were cheering her on.
she felt like herself again.

the inner alignment that she searched for
outside herself
was emerging from within.
she could easily tune into her body
and listen.
now, she doesn't feel tempted
or swayed
to do anything that will take away
from this beautiful inner balance.

van ekeren

chapter three

poet in residence

poet in residence

love yourself enough
to generate the words
that support your growth
and make you feel safe.
learn how to make this a habit.
gently craft the ongoing narrative
that will shape your inner world.
understand that your mindset
is yours to shape and mold.

the poet in residence is
writing their life
in real time.
they do not change their truth
for the comfort of others.
they boldly proclaim their sense of self
on each page of their story.

they have the ability
to sculpt today's pain into
tomorrow's possibilities.
they trust life
even when it feels hopeless.
prophesizing the beauty in all things
begins to feel natural to this poet.

they are not swayed by the external
because their interal heartbeat
is the only rhythm to which they abide to.

**love yourself enough
to generate the words
that support your growth.**

the design of it all

the life you have lived up until now
has informed and educated you.
if you are not living the life you want to live,
take this wisdom
and seek something different.
what can you do to become
the person you want to be?
how can you see her more clearly?

design your future
rather than assess the damage of what's been.
the past has happened,
and the future is waiting for you to create it.

breathe in fully.
exhale the breath.
let this momentum signal
how to let go
of the past.
your mind is waiting for you to
design and transform it.

write a thank you letter to yourself

when the momentum of life
begins to feel haphazard,
take a moment to be present with yourself.
feel whatever it is
that you have been running from.
face your inner fear
and trauma.
rather than let it bounce
on the surface of your mind,
invite it in.
you are ready to go there.
instead of categorizing trauma as tragic,
what if you saw it as an invitation to become?
life will be painful.
life will hurt.
accept it all.
let your guard down,
stop analyzing your pain
and just sit with it.
you are not a bad person
for feeling this way.
in fact, you are courageous
to meet yourself here.
you have been running from this feeling
for quite some time.

you are with it now.
it cannot hurt you
when you are present with it.
your conscious intention
will always be more powerful
than unconscious fear.
know this.
let your life
be a love letter to yourself.
you are boldly
on this journey toward
your most fulfilling self.
you are becoming
you.

**let your life
be a love letter
to yourself.**

know your why

when you know your why,
you know your purpose.
you know why you create what you do
and your work feels meaningful.
you are not easily distracted
by temporary attention or accolades.
when you know your why,
you're not thrown off course
if others do not applaud your work.
life just feels
more nourishing and fun
when you know your purpose.

pain becomes art

i used to hide my pain
because i thought it showed weakness.
i wanted to create a facade
that i shared with the world
that appeared glossy and tidy.
i was not willing to be vulnerable in ways
that felt too personal.
the thought of inviting someone in
to see how i hurt
felt paralyzing.
how could i be loved if i showed pain?
how would i be perceived?
holding in the intensity of pain
always seems to prompt more pain.
i discovered that i had to open up.

the process of sharing
the shadows of my pain started slowly.
i would speak in metaphors
and then in specifics.
after praciticing this art,
i began to feel free.
everything that i had looked for externally
was at my immediate grasp from within.

my pain could inform my art
and connect me to the people
that were like me.
i could write about it.
i could share it all
on a deeper level.
admitting my pain has helped me
become more of me.

the force that animates you

when life feels so good to live,
you have aligned with the forces within.
you have faced the trauma in your life
and chose to transmute it.
you have decided to love yourself
in the midst of everything.
you have bestowed abundant grace
upon all aspects of your existence.
you have given up the habit of self hatred
and are not triggered to return
to this way of life.
you understand that the culture
may try to sway you off balance,
but you work everyday to stay aligned.
you enjoy this work.

this inner force that animates your life
is your focus.
you speak to it
and through it.
you enjoy its unconditional love
and try to merge with this jovial essence.
you are beginning to understand
that your relationship with yourself
and this invisible force
is where true creation happens.

73

you get to collaborate with the divine.
your inner and external worlds
nourish one another.
life feels poetic to live.

you are never missing out

you're never missing out
on anything
when you love who you are.

you're never missing out
on anything
when you're living in your truth.

you're never missing out
on anything
when you're creating the life you value.

you're never missing out
on anything
when you're going in your own direction.

honor who you are and how you've gotten here.
respect everyone around you,
but do not think you need to emulate them
to show love.
love yourself and your personal journey.
tend to your own garden
before offering to help another.
as you become more transparent
in who you are,
your life will open up in magical ways.

plant the seeds

when you plant the seeds
in the invisible world,
your intentions will be felt.
the ripple effect
of your healthy ideas
will eventually take shape.
things will sprout in your outer life
when you continue to develop
your inner life.
determine what you want.
act as if you already have it.
your dreams
have been summoned
when you reach for them.
have patience and trust
that forces greater than you
are working in your favor.

when you stop ignoring

something changes
when you stop ignoring
the signals from your body.
you begin to align
and shift from a state of anxiety
to excitement.
you connect and tune into your body and mind
and feel something special.
you are no longer running away
from these signs and messages.
you are surrendering to them.
it's as if the sun is rising from within
and illuminating everything that was dark.

you understand that
this internal conversation
will never end
because night follows day.
you get to run into the shadows
openly and willingly
knowing that you eventually will be able to see.
this is when your true life begins.
you get to open up to life
in the ways that you have always wanted to.
you get to trust yourself again.

you feel like you are
creating poetry again.
you get to truly live
and give your whole heart
to it all.

offline poet

it is that moment in your story
when you understand the value
of your attention.
you realize that you had been
giving it away
to aspects of life that did not concern you.
you had been focusing
on the wrong things.
it is that moment
when this awakening crystallizes
and you choose to focus your attention
on the real world
in front of you.
you go offline
to truly live.
you tune out
to tune in.

it is when you choose intention
over external attention.
your values
are creating your character.
this is your life's work
as your character
is your fate.

the lure of the wrong things,
the fear of missing out
and the drive to appear a certain way
fade with the smoothness of a setting sun.
there is no inner battle
because the soul wants what's good for it.
this new and refreshing boundary
that you've created
just feels right.
you can now feel the calm
that you hoped the external world
would provide for you.
you can connect with yourself
on a pure level.
you no longer need to prove
who you are
to yourself
or anyone else.

van ekeren

chapter four

blue jean era

blue jean era

it is that feeling when
you feel comfortable in your mind and body.
you just know who you are.
you enjoy being around others
because you enjoy your own company.
life feels lighter and friendlier.
you have decided to embark upon it all
with a jovial spirit.
you know this will not always be easy,
but you are dedicated to its pursuit.

clad in your blue jeans,
you state your presence.
you do not take things to seriously,
yet live out your values.
you are the yin and yang of it all.
you love a good solid laugh,
yet are always willing to go deep on any topic.
you're in it.
you are creating your life in real time.
you seek out style, but never exclusivity.
life's offerings
should be open to everyone.
because you believe this,
you are willing to pursue
the things that matter to you.

just be open to it all

open up your heart to life.
drink it all in.
the ups, the downs
and the in between moments.
mess up.
fall.
fail.
pick yourself back up.
let others see all parts of you.
just remember that
another's words
or reactions
having nothing to do with you.
you decide who you are
and who you want to be.
your life is up to you.
go create something special.
have fun and don't forget
to laugh at yourself.

the simplicity of focus

when you choose to focus on
the true work that you need to do
to be you,
you will see the path with clear eyes.
the distractions that used to loom around
and fog your vision
suddenly disappear.
the simplicity of focus
sharpens every muscle in your mind.
you feel aligned,
yet calm.
your being feels energized
and peaceful.

this growth is a personal luxury
available to us all.
it is an investment in yourself to
become curious about the pain
that lingers within your body.
you are the only one who feels it
and can sense it.
sit with it
and learn from it.
become the custom tailor
to your entire inner world.

change the measurements to
make everything feel just right.
take your time
with these inner alterations.

if you have been avoiding it,
look directly at it.
pause.
change your reaction.
repeat this simple approach
and be patient with yourself.
you are creating haute couture
with the fabric that you were given.
you are changing the culture
because you are changing your culture.

**courage
is an approach to life.**

infuse courage

courage
is an approach to life.
courage ignites an inner power.
it's a way to infuse everyday decisions
with an intention and a goal.
courage
will open up doors you never imagined
walking through.
it elevates your mood
and reminds you that this is it.
this is your own life to create
and thrive in.
courage needs you
as much as you need it.
vow to be brave.
feel this feeling throughout
your entire body.
surrender to your strength
and trust it.
you only need to believe
in yourself
to create something special
with your life.

developing self reverence

i used to think that
i needed another's gaze
to ignite my worth.
as i learn how to develop
self reverence,
i am facing the harsh inner critic—
the young girl inside of me
that felt alone
and ashamed at times in her life.
i am sitting with her
and not running from her.
she is needy,
yet i am not fearful of her.
i am reprogramming this need
into excitement.
it is a level of energy
that is easily transmutable
with practice and focus.
i get to be in charge
of my inner world.
self love is self reverence.
it is creating joy out of thin air.
it is breathing in with honor
and exhaling with thoughtful wisdom.
everything seems so clear
when i value myself.

self love is self reverence.

that casual cool vibe in jeans and a white t-shirt

it is showing up in your favorite
white t-shirt and jeans
and letting this tone present your energy.
it is that casual cool vibe
that just makes you feel more like yourself.
knowing this can be your home frequency,
you rest into this mindset
and let it happen unconsciously.
you just feel like yourself.
this ease and knowing beckons
like minds and souls.
your calm style signals others
to relax into theirs as well.
confidence in style is contagious.
be iconic in this simple uniform.
exude something that not everyone else has.
let your casual cool vibe
in your t-shirt and jeans
manifest in all areas of your life.
you're present, yet chill.
you're energetic, yet at peace.
you're able to carry yourself
and find a spot at any table
in this look.

**it is that casual cool vibe
that makes you feel more
like yourself.**

just knowing

knowing that
who you are today
is exactly enough.
settling into this.

creating goals
from this safe space.
soaking up the abundance
of this sense of self.

seeing yourself
as beautifully unique.
basking in this truth
that your presence
is always enough.

the flicker of something new

it has been there,
waiting for me to see it.
there is a flicker,
an awakening,
an inner nudge
that feels new.
it patiently hovered in the background
of my mind.
it took time for me to trust in the new
rather than rely on old habits.
what if i let trust guide me?
what i let my old habits go?
there is truly nothing to lose
in trying.
as i acknowledge this
blossoming inner glow,
i can fan the flame.
happiness feels within reach.

your favorite t-shirt

the nostalgic feeling
that your favorite t-shirt
summons from your soul.

the soft cotton against your skin,
the comfortable patina of the fabric,
the nostalgia of this fit
that reminds you of yourself.

paired with your worn out jeans
that hug your body perfectly,
you feel nostalgically confident.
it is an old feeling laced with new vigor.
the memories within this piece of clothing
exude and encapsulate
your best self.

the simplicity and style
of your blue jeans and an old t-shirt
comfort and excite you.
it resurrects your most confident version
of yourself.
the alchemy that occurs
when you slip into this simple uniform
awakens you.

95

**you feel
nostalgically confident.**

yesterday happened so today could

yesterday happened.
it is now over
and you get to be you today.
can you let the past go
so you can be present?
allow the good to surface from all things
and then let the rest go.
understand that you will never be perfect
and choose to adore this aspect
of being human.
honor and revere
everything about you.
look back on the ups and downs
with a simple mind.
let go of any connections
to suffering as a way of life.
you may have thought
that this was a safe way to deflect pain,
but it creates more of it.

cling to joy.
be transparent
as you traverse this focus.
flex your mind muscle
to see the gift of today.

97

practice this.
enjoy the experience
of it all
because you are
adorable and
perfectly imperfect.

the work of sadness

the next time that you feel sad,
see it as a cue to get to work.
notice this lower energetic frequency
and pause.
it is time to ask yourself
why you feel what you're feeling.
what is really bothering you?
it is time to get to work
on being honest with yourself.

rather than being afraid of sadness,
embrace it.
when you notice it
and treat it as an alert system,
you can think more clearly.
you are able to assess the sadness
and fully comprehend it.

remember your abundant capabilities
when you work in the present moment.
you do not need to guard yourself
against future sadness
because you know that you can handle it
in the moment.

you become comfortable
in the present moment
because it feels safe.
you have created the safe space
within any feeling
by trusting in yourself and your abilities.

that perfect wave

just as sidhartha discovers
that wisdom must be learned
and not taught,
a sense of self
is learned and discovered.
when you experience humility,
when you fall down and get back up,
when you truly feel pain and joy,
and when you show up over and over again,
you are merging with your true self.
this naive willingness
feels good.
you are not afraid to share who you are
and let others see you.
your style exudes from your inner world.
you feel proud to be who you are.
there is a magical quality
experienced when you feel like yourself.
you no longer need drama
to spark attention.
your inner spark drives you.
the ease of your lifestyle
is like that of a surfer riding that perfect wave.

**a sense of self
is learned and discovered.**

102

chapter five

she speaks
in poems

she speaks in poems

to create her world,
she speaks in poems.
she works to see the good
and knows that this intention
will always guide her.
she grows with grit and determination
and shares with excitement.
she reaches toward herself
over and over again.
she trusts
and is willing to be vulnerable.
her passionate commitment
to see the poetry in all things
continually awakens her soul.
she never feels fear
because she syncs up with the
benevolent forces in the world.

she is waking up to herself

as the invisible cues in nature
signal birth and growth,
she listens to her unique inner compass.
she understands that she has access
to something larger than her—
a knowing,
a feeling
and a special connection.
it feels like coming home
when she can tap into this magnificent force.
she remembers
and forgets
with no inner judgment.
life will never be perfect
nor will she be.
she is a radiant being
waking up to her potential.
her unique perspective
and expansive spirit
guide from within.
things are just beginning for her.

she's an old soul poet

it is the way that she carries herself,
you feel like you know her.
she holds the space for your pain
yet doesn't focus on it.
she gives you a feeling of safety and soaring
all at once.
you can sense that she tries to do this
for herself.
she has been through pain,
but she sees struggle as the catalyst
to create something new.
the old pain is alchemized on today's canvas.
she's an old soul poet
collecting ways in which to live and to love.
feeling her passion and reverence toward
change and growth inspires you.
you can see how
it is an honor to be an old soul.
it allows you to be any age.
she seems to abide by her own unique set of
values that have been defined
several times over.
you are not afraid
to live at your greatest depth
because of her.

**the old pain is alchemized
on today's canvas.**

her imagination

she can easily
turn inward
toward her imagination
and envision a dream,
a creation
or a new idea to an old problem
at any given moment.
she knows how to continually
cultivate her imagination.
she can always feel the good
overcoming the bad.
she just knows
who she is
and how to imagine the good.

engage in new material

even if it is not
in your wheelhouse
reach out for something new.
cast a wide net.
read something new,
be around new people
and try to understand
what they're going through.
look at art
that triggers you.
engage in something new
even if it feels uncomfortable at the moment.

she will not settle

as she chooses to narrate
and define her own set of values,
her integrity and resilience
will be challenged.
the culture wants her to stay the same,
to acquiesce,
to listen to others
and to feel fear
if she's not immediately accepted.
she is keenly aware
of the culture's pull.
it has tugged on her heart
and led her astray before.
she is becoming wise and unapologetic.
she is ready to soar.
eager to become
and to transform,
she will not settle
for what fear and anxiety want
to produce in her.
she is willing to sit with the discomfort
to emerge as her fullest self.
the temptations will always be there
to give up
or to feel shame or doubt,

but she can see through them.
without hanging onto their intensity,
these fears eventually fade away.
with practice, she can breathe
through anything.
she uses momentum to sharpen her clarity
and allows experiences to
infuse her inner wisdom.
her curiosity and wonder
seem to attract unthinkable possibilities.
she is tapped in
and ready to go.

**because she reaches,
she is reached toward.**

she is poetry

because she tries,
she succeeds.
because she shows up for herself,
she is growing.
because she puts in the work,
she feels more like herself.
because she cares,
she is supported.
because she reaches,
she is reached toward.
because she is learning to see,
she does not get distracted.
because she is listening
to her inner guidance,
she enjoys the idea of discipline.
because she sees herself,
others can see her.
because,
she
is poetry.

the lure of the inner critic

the life you dream about
lies inside you now.
it is quietly within you
waiting to be discovered
as is your outspoken inner critic.
both coexist in your mind.
you have the means
to turn down the volume of the critical voice
at any moment.
when you are truly present in the moment
and continue to put yourself out there
in new ways,
this inner critic can only whisper.
you are not under its spell
nor need to bargain with it.
you get to identify it,
admit it
and then get past it.
this voice will get louder
when you try to ignore it.
it will pull you in
with every trick it can think of.
the lure of its magnitude appears larger
than it is.

use the energy spent running
from this voice
to rewrite it.
open up to embodying
a form of self trust
that does not have to be earned.
experience the new emotions of
loving yourself.
flex this muscle.
feel this abundant joy.
this inner critic
can become your best friend.

she meets herself

she continues
to rediscover herself
in all aspects of her life.
rather than identify with each thought,
mannerism
or behavior that she exhibits,
she observes them
with grace and reverence.
after all,
she is watching
her entire life's work unfold.
her entire being
is her own creation.
she is a product of herself.
as she watches herself,
she can choose which aspects
that she wants to enhance
and those that she wants to let go.
this magical process
sheds the skin that no longer suits her
and awakens inner growth.
she is cultivating and curating
her entire being.
moment by moment
this joyful process lures her in.

she is so excited
to continue meeting herself
in new ways
for the rest of her beautiful life.

poetry is

poetry is
trying to share a good feeling
with a stranger
and hoping that it elevates
their inner narrative.
it is rebranding the pain,
the challenges
and the struggles that life brings us.
it is embracing the failures
and rewriting these experiences.

poetry is
contemplating the human experience.
it is shining a light
on the habits that hurt
and working to replace them
with something new.

poetry is
seeing the art
that is always around you.
it is understanding
that pain
and fear
are both art.

they shape you into
something new.

poetry is
knowing that you have the last say
in how pain
sculpts you.
it is seeing challenges
as the magic
that weaves
our entire human experience together.

she gets lost in art

the way it moves her
and gives her access to depths within
and around.
it is similar to the feeling that a song
can generate
that brings her back
to a specific moment of joy.
the beauty within
is ignited when she gets lost in art.
it inspires her
to create,
share
and become more of herself.
getting lost in art
restores her soul.
this soothing feeling
reminds her of
jumping into a calm pool
as the warm water engulfs her entire body.
she surrenders to the moment.
she feels so alive
in this visceral experience.

**the beauty within is ignited
when she gets lost in art.**

just start enjoying it all

the good,
the bad,
the joy,
the fear
and all of the rest—
just start enjoying it all.

eventually,
after enough time,
it all seems
like poetry.
one day in the future,
you will look back on most things
with fondness,
reverence
and admiration.

being human
is a journey through the extremes.
pain, joy, rest and work.
let each moment,
as intense or soft as it may be,
make you better.

just set the intention

to start enjoying it all
and letting it make you better.
when you surrender to life,
you ignite something deep inside of you.
trust comes naturally
and your perspective lights your way.

let the algorithms pass you
by because you are too busy
living your precious life.

momentum is life

action creates
your next action.
moving, becoming, growing
and changing
are the key elements to life.
overextend
rather than stay safe.
put yourself in more situations
that feel awkward.
let this be your new superpower.
crave something that's new and different.
develop into someone
who is original and unique.
let the algorithms pass you by
because you are too busy living
your precious life.

face it

face the thing
that is fogging your vision.
accept and acknowledge your inabilities
and work on them.
laugh at yourself
and your past mistakes.
give yourself a hug.
take a deep breath.
breathe in the air
and feel its love.
you are living in a dream.
your dream.
untangle yourself from anything
that does not support your best self.
do the work this calls for.
disassociate from those
who are not good for you.
be strong enough to choose yourself
over and over again.
define what matters to you
and go after it.
let your life be really good.
know that the work
works.
just put in the time
and wait for the magical results.

let your decisions guide you

create confidence
through your decision making process.
feel into every choice
and why you're making it.
discover and polish your intuition.
remember to honor this ability.
making a choice
gives your entire being energy.
learn how to gain perspective
through this momentum.
the end result of any decision
is not always under your control.
try your best
and know
that this is enough.
your decisions are yours.
honor the act of making a choice.
honor yourself.
let this energy
lead your way.

chapter six

life is a
mood board

let your life be a mood board

let it all be inspirational
and add to the collective tapestry of your life.
let each moment inform the next.
when you are aware and present,
the cohesive beauty of life
will be able to find you and take root.

the power of the present moment
is your medium.
your entire life is your work of art.
the small journeys take you just as far
as the longer ones.
you wander with eyes wide open
and an eagerness to see.
you discover everything in real time
because you are not overthinking.

you are letting the flow of life
show you the way.
the simplicity of your truth
excites you.
as you tap into this childlike wonder,
you understand true beauty—
it is the art of being alive.

trust your art

create openly
and wildly.
trust the process.
trust in your art.
let your creations
connect you
to deeper parts within.
see your work
with kind eyes
and an open heart.
discover more of you
in your art.
let it
just be.
create without a need
for others to appreciate it.
let the act of creating
be the reward.

the beginning

the beginning
is actually the middle
because
it means that you made a decision
to start something new.
you're halfway there
when you intentionally make a change.
you've focused your energy
in a new way.
you're able to synthesize wisdom
to generate
the outcome you want
with ease.
sometimes,
the decision will eventually
become the outcome.
the goal is reached
when it is defined.

honor your entire being

slow down
to be with yourself.
pause and reflect
and rediscover
everything about you.
breathe into your purest confidence.
this is living.
this is your life.
you are everything that you seek.
your heart is the one
that you want.
honor your entire being.
be with it.
be present in your environment.
go on a walk outside
regarldess of the weather.
be completely present
as your feet touch the ground.
feel grateful to hear your footsteps.
honor the entire experience.
let this reverent song
be your approach toward life.

keep creating it

act like you are living
the life that you are dreaming of.
keep creating the feelings
this life would conjure up within you.
feel these feelings.
experience these feelings.
let your beautiful dream life
merge with this moment.

observe yourself within this dream life.
breathe deep into it.
honor the body and mind
that's taken you here.
you are choosing joy
and declaring it all as simple, fun
and even easy.

difficulty is only a measurement.
you don't have to succumb to its pull.
life is simple when you set a goal
and reach toward it.
let the goal
be the biggest dream you can imagine.

thriving is contagious

one of the best feelings
in the world is
watching
someone you love
thrive.
their joy
feels like your joy.
you are bonded by
this magical thread of connection.
you understand
that to thrive
is to feel as if you've succeeded.
know that this feeling
is always accessible.
be proud of yourself
for getting through
any challenge.
let the
"getting through" part
signify success.
when you open up to this feeling
and reach for it,
it reaches back.
let yourself thrive.

**sharing your heart
is powerful.**

sharing your heart

if you feel your best
when you share your heart
and your love,
lean into this.
this is who you are.
learn to share with conviction,
strength and integrity.
use your own energy
to combat any lower energy
that may be lurking around you
or in others.

sharing your heart is powerful
amd will guide you to the right places.
it will make you feel like you.
this is your gift to the world.

there will be ups and downs,
but remember who you are.
you are a loving and joyful human.
lean into this.
keep sharing.
rise up to each moment
with the most love you can give.

the life of an observer

writing down your thoughts,
feelings
and experiences
helps you detach from it all
and see clearly.
you start to observe the beautiful journey
you've been on
with eyes of reverence.
you can see
yourself
for the first time.
this sparks eternal self love
and respect.
you are honored to be you.
you are curious and intrigued by your life
and so proud of yourself.
how exactly did you get here?
how did you overcome so much?
it feels good
to see
without judgement
and admire the life
you've lived.
the future looks so bright and exciting.
anything is possible
when you are not scared.

you just know
that you can handle anything
because
you already have done so.

patience and momentum

there is momentum
in patience.
as you paint the background
and prep for the foreground,
life is filling in all the spaces
and nuances
to support the best possible outcome.
as you create a clear picture of what you want,
you carefully curate
the outcome.
you have to reach for things
and you have to wait for things.
both are equally as magical.

the now

dropping into the now
is a skill.
like all skills,
you can learn it,
practice it
and then get better at it.
you are able to be present
and appreciate it all.
what a wonderful experience
this life is
when you can find the heart of it.
the core of your existence
truly lies in being present.
this feeling resides in all of us
at any given moment.
it is learning how to access it
and live within it.
it is accepting yourself
today, exactly as you are,
while joyfully surrendering to a life
of growing and changing.

writing the script

your life is the story that you create
and recreate everyday.
you are writing the script
of the movie that you star in.
be the main character.
feel the way that you want to.
create the character
that you are proud to be.
rest into your narrative
and trust your ability to do so.

back in the flow of it all

sometimes
you have to step back
and remove yourself from the flow.
you just know
that this private time
will nourish you more
than seeking your position externally.
it is not something to be feared
or ashamed of,
it is a call to action
within.
it is knowing
that some shifts are occurring
and you need personal space and time
to honor them.
some internal moments
do not need to be explained in real time.
soak them up.
be with them.
return to the flow when you are ready.
it will always be waiting for you.

to create from peace

to create from a place of peace and gratitude
frees you from the pain of the past.
you are using your mind muscle
to make something new.
you no longer need to
ruminate on the past.
settling into this sustainable peace
takes initiative
and the ability to face your truth.
it means sitting in the discomfort
that you have been running from.
this peaceful mindset is yours
when you reach for it.
this blissful and wholesome feeling
may take some time to inhabit.
trust that your intention to feel it
activates magical forces within you.
the will
becomes the way.
the map to get there
is located within.
to create from this peace
allows you to separate yourself
from unhealthy goals.

a peaceful mind
can generate the miracles
that your heart dreams of.
when you feel this inner peace,
you are not tempted to follow
in another's footsteps
because you know
that the only way for you
is yours.

van ekeren

chapter seven

to romanticize life

**you are writing the story
of your life
in real time.**

always young

let the life you create
keep you young.
be happy with
exactly where you're at.
stop comparing and
enjoy your own growth.

build upon a foundation
of love and courage.
no problem is ever
too big for you because
you see through the lens of hope.

know that pain is a part of life
and accept that you cannot control
all aspects of your environment.
understand that
true self-confidence emerges
from within.

when your inner compass speaks

the sound of your intuition
takes time to connect with
and hear.
your inner compass
does not use language,
but it speaks in other ways.
seek its wisdom
and trust that you will receive it.
lean in
and rest in this truth.
you may not get detailed instructions
on what to do,
but you will just know.
you'll know who you are
and what direction you're going.
you'll know what feeling good
feels like.
when your inner compass
speaks to you,
honor the information it sends.
you will soon make sense of it all,
but for now,
just allow.

the version of you

the version of yourself
that you are now
is joyfully imperfect.
she is beautiful and strong
and has carried you this far.
adore her.
cherish her.
honor her.
she has been working in your favor
for many years.
this version of who you are
is breathtakingly confident.
she is thriving in her truth.
she is savoring each aspect of her life.
she is not perfect,
no one is.
she does not hold back.
she presents herself as the
beautiful, healthy and strong woman
that she knows she is.

seeing life as a poem

a poet is an artist
trying to create something better
with what they already have.
an emotion,
a feeling,
an intuition,
and a reflection
are the raw ingredients of their work.
the poet
is a champion of trying—
trying to see the world with open eyes.
the poet
creates beauty from pain
and understands that one's life
is being created through the words
she uses to describe it.
this writer acknowledges the truth,
then tries to rework and reshape
her role within it all.
her objective is to be at peace within.
she knows that her work is special
because it is changing her world.
it's changing her life.
she knows that as she changes herself,
the people around her begin to change as well.

153

there's a synergy and excitement
that infuses everything she does.
she awakens with excitement each morning
to do this work.
seeing life as a continual poem
will always generate hope
and connect her to her most fulfilling self.

style is what you are

the way you integrate
the little things
into your life
is style.
it is how you wear your
most comfortable t-shirt and jeans.
it is how you order your morning coffee
at your favorite coffee shop.
style is what you are.
it is the life force
that connects you to the right people
as well as the guiding light
that tells you where to go next.
if you are in doubt
or feeling less confident than usual,
reach toward your style.
let its poetic song
shape your day.

your story

you are writing the story
of your life
in real time.
you carefully narrate
your inner world
trying to be more kind to yourself
with each day.
your story may take turns
that you weren't expecting,
but you ultimately shape the narrative.
you get to choose to be excited
and open to each new day.
you lean into the work needed
to keep discovering
and learning.
you continually write
the character that you want to be.
your goal is to be flexible
and grateful
with all things that life gives you.
you are always the main character
of your story.

brooklyn breeze

that gentle summer wind
evokes gratitude, playfulness and joy.
it feels like the world was made for us
as we stroll through our neighborhood.
the summer is coming to an end soon
and life just feels simple.
the brooklyn breeze brings insightful reflection
on personal values that we are working on.
as we walk,
we talk.
we remember the work that we have done
and the people who have helped us.
we feel grateful for it all.
another summer is coming to an end.
the rhythm of nature
shares her wisdom with us.
there is time to play
and time to work.
we vow to soak up each moment
and celebrate our existence.
the breeze will always feel soft and gentle
when we are kind to ourselves.

your life

the life that you are curating
is yours.
make it bold.
feel brave.
if you have a goal,
define it
so you can reach it.
your precious life is living within you.
declare it.
find the rising tide
to lift you.
put yourself around
the right people.
believe in yourself
so much that you wake up smiling
because
you get to be you.

the moments

the examined life
leads to the revered life.
when you look back on the moments
of your life,
you can see how the hardest experiences
shaped you
into who you are now.
this beautiful soul inside of you
is continually learning how to communicate
with your mind.

pain, fear, insecurity
and other similar feelings
can be transmuted into something beautiful.
challenges help you see
with eyes of optimism.
the hard moments
demand something from you.
you have had to learn,
to grow
and change.
the moments that you feared the most
helped sculpt you
into the person that you are today.

**believe in yourself so much
that you wake up smiling
because you get to be you.**

your response

life is not about what happens to you,
it is about how you respond to it all.
let life happen
through you.
do not fight it.
allow your reactions to surface.
pause and think through how you would like
your entire being to respond.
this pause
and reflection
will become your new life.
you will begin to not fear anything
because
you know how to keep it together within.
the space between a reaction and a response
will ignite self trust and confidence.
even if your external world is chaotic,
you can imbue calmness and peace
onto any situation.
this new sense of bravery will
open up your life
in new ways.

**this new sense of bravery
will open up your life
in new ways.**

golden hour

when you approach each moment
as cinematic,
life has a way of delivering this sentiment.
the forgiving tones of the sky at golden hour
create the color palette of your mindset.
golden hues, soft pastels and rich light
embody your inner world.
you have chosen to see the art within
and all around you.
every moment is golden hour
and you just want to bask in it.
the concept of gratitude
sings with the brushstrokes of the sun
in the setting sky.
the reassurance that the sun will come back
awakens your ability to feel safe.
you are alive.
you are in this moment.
let the golden hour
paint the rest of your experiences
with its emblamatic highlights.

intentionally iconic

every iconic figure
has a similar origin story.
one that is rooted in self belief
and self trust.
this elevated sense of self,
this joyful exuberance,
this way of being begins on the inside.
it is not reliant on achievements
or popularity,
it is how you carry yourself in the good times
and in the bad.
it is feeling so good
in your own mind and body
that you are completely present.
you genuinely care about yourself and others.
you do not need to look too far ahead
because you know that small daily decisions
matter more than luck.
when you set an intention
to be your own icon,
you will get there.
stay focused, get out of your own way
and take risks.
you will feel iconic, yet vulnerable,
and life will seem to continually
roll out the red carpet for you.

letting life love you

when you learn how to love all parts of
yourself, you fall in love with life.
as you love life more,
it seems to love you back.
this benevolent bond feels like
heaven on earth.

getting to this internal peace
was a challenge.
the wounded parts of you lashed out.
the road toward happiness
felt dark and heavy at times.

despite it all, you kept going.
you kept moving toward love.
you reached inside your heart
and asked for help.

slowly, the urge to protect yourself
from your wounded self faded.
you began to surrender to peace.
you chose love.
you know that you will always love yourself
while life loves you back.

**as you love life more,
it seems to love you back.**

to romanticize life

the poet's calling is
to romanticize life.
the rich colors, moods and moments
have brought you to this day.
the pain and pleasure of the past
have served a purpose.
you are free to exist in the moment
and yield to the power of today.

just as the keys of the piano
patiently wait to be played,
your life is openly waiting
for you to mold it.
your present mindset sets the tone
for how you see.

the possibilities of tomorrow
await your gaze.
you continue to craft your lens
and mindset.
you vow to
keep doing the inner work
in order to support your outer growth.

to romanticize your life
is to see through
the rose colored lens
and make poetry out of it all,
no matter what.
you vow to write a new poem each day
and go live it.

van ekeren

about the author

Nikki Van Ekeren is a writer and an artist.

Her work is rooted in optimisim, self-growth, and celebrating one's self.

Nikki's other books include *Grace & Grit*, *Palm Trees and Possibilities*, *Poems on Style*, *Happy Hour Poetry*, and for children, *You Get to Be You*.